THE CONTROLLERS

A VIEW OF OUR RESPONSIBILITY

By JIM COLE

Illustrated by Tom Woodruff

Published by Jim Cole
37- Lomita Dr.
Mill Valley, Calif.
94941

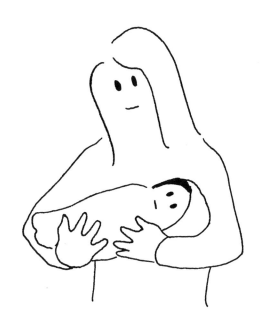

At first I was held and
completely cared for.

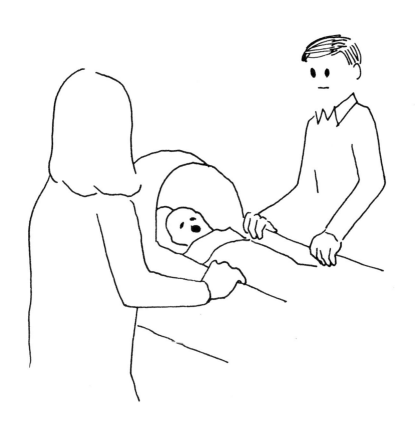

I was helpless and could not
control myself so they
decided everything for me.

When I did something,
someone else took the
responsibility

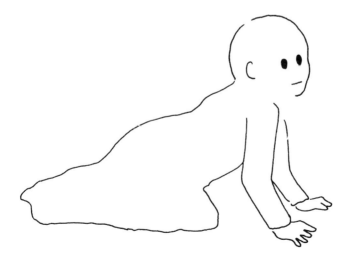

because they had
control over me.

Slowly their control
became less complete

People expected me to do things that I didn't want to do

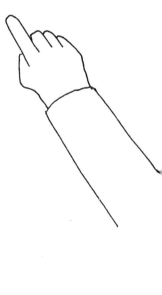

and I was afraid to say,
"I don't want to."

So I developed controllers

and I gave the controllers
the responsibility.

No one can see my controllers

so I tell people about them.

Often I tell people about
my controllers in little ways.

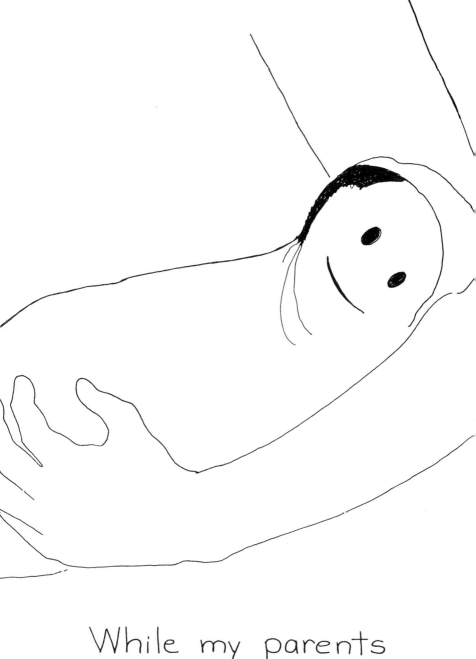

While my parents
were warm, close, and
certain in their control,

the new controllers are not.

The controllers are not really with me so they don't bring much comfort.

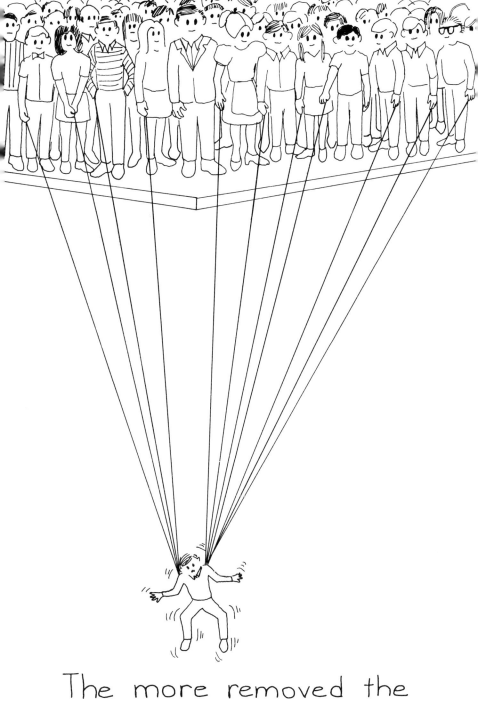

The more removed the
controllers are from me
the more of them I need

and the more uncertain
I feel.

To overcome my uncertainty, I spend most of my time looking for new controllers.

I have many ways of
getting new controllers.

Sometimes after I have
already done something,
I look for a controller.

But I often let him know that I have made him responsible for my feelings.

Sometimes I try to give someone my controls

and I feel helpless.

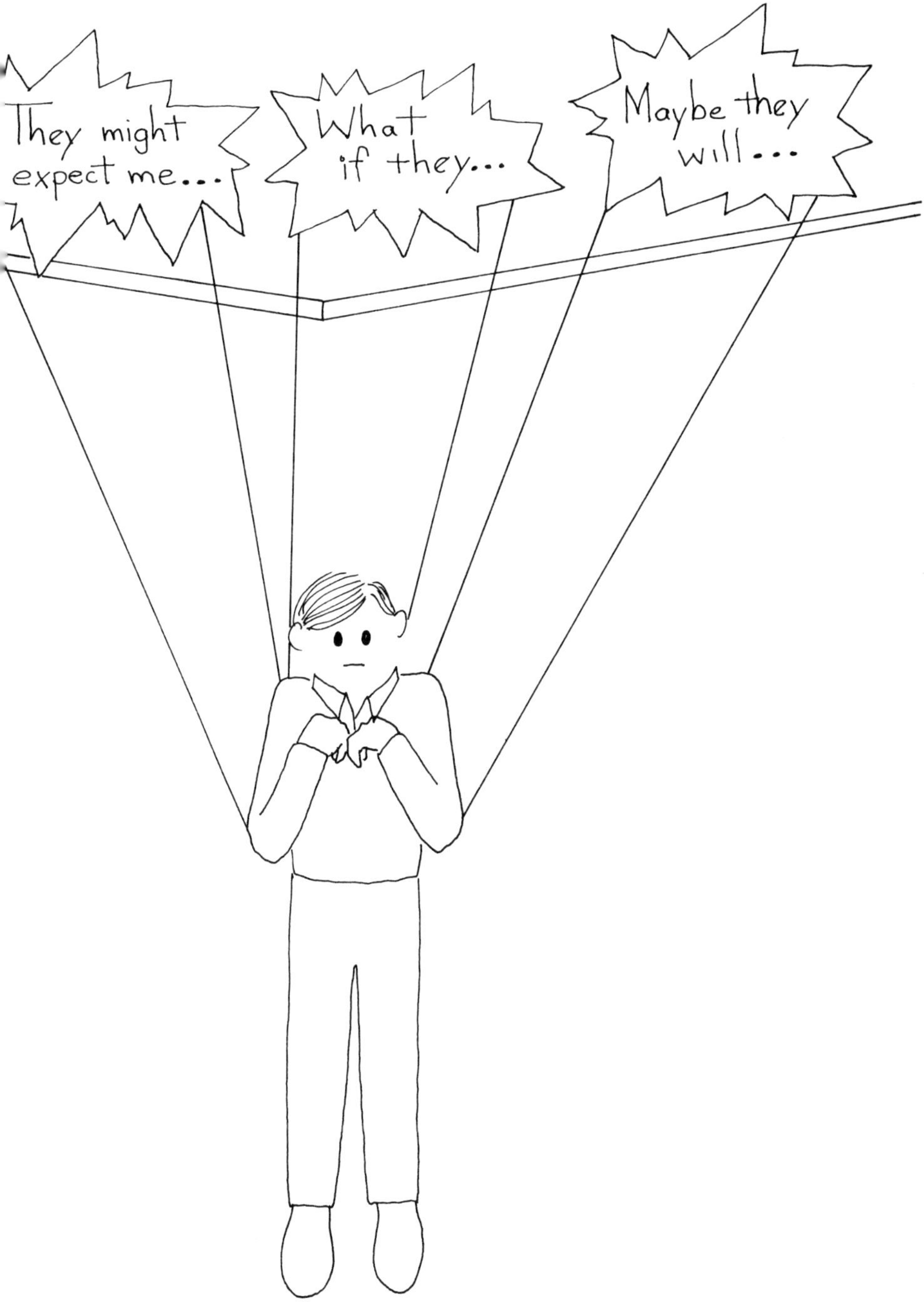

so I build controllers of what I'm afraid they will want.

The controllers I make of fears don't comfort me

so I comfort myself
with controllers from
my past.

While I am looking for controllers I am afraid to change my behavior.

Sometimes I become
frightened and yell
for help.

Someone tries to help
me become free from
my controllers

and I make him a
controller.

I spend a lot of time telling myself I'm controlled.

While I'm complaining about my controllers

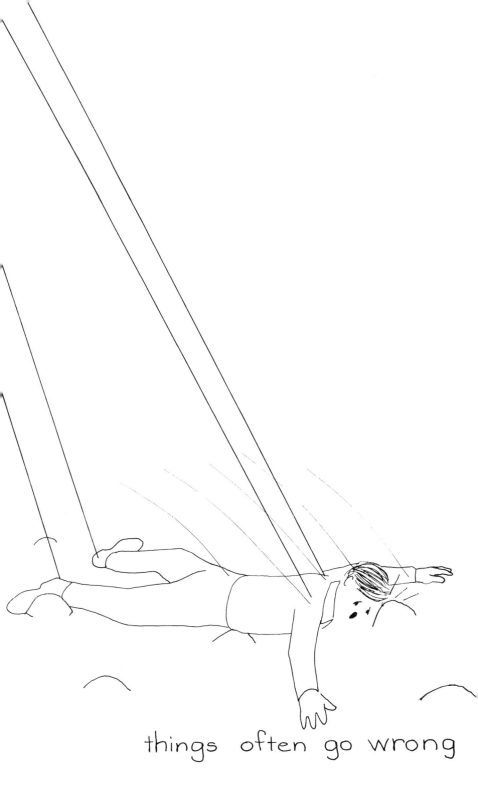

things often go wrong

and it's all
their fault.

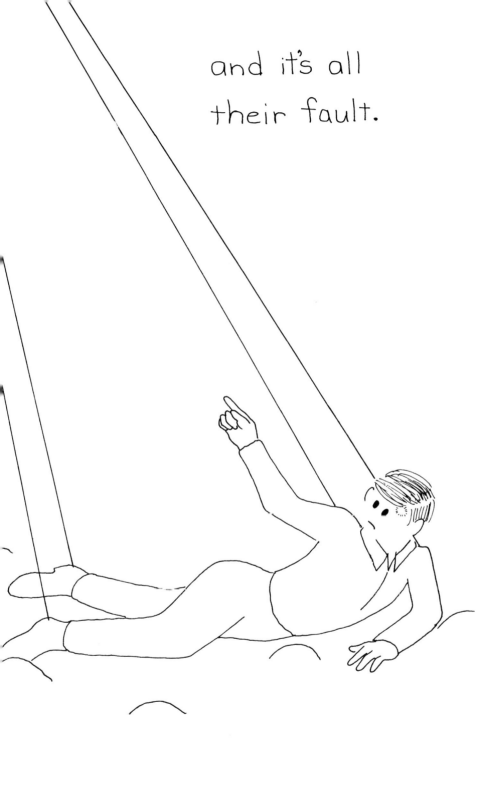

Sometimes I'm

under real pressure

but the pressure
does not have
control of me.

Only if I make
it my controller does the
pressure have control of me.

Then I work to keep the pressure in control.

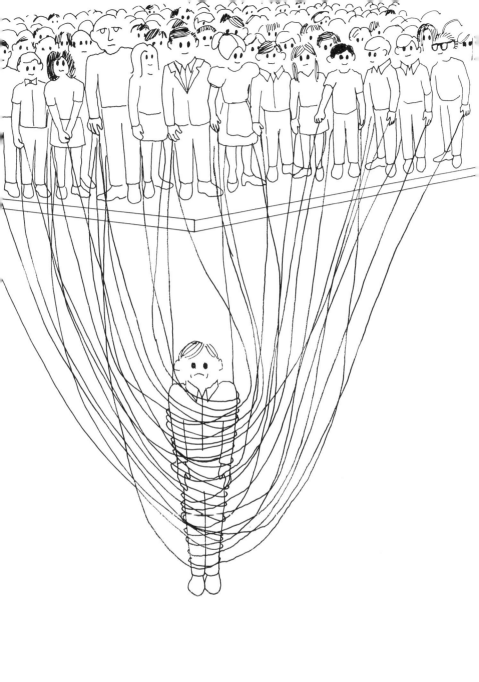

I often feel very restricted
by the controllers.

I forget that I created
the controllers and I decide
who will be responsible.

Sometimes I know I am responsible for what I have done.

Then I see my controllers

and the
controllers get
the credit.

So I become a controller
to get the credit.

When the other person falls,
I get hurt

and I get
blamed.

I can not control others and be free myself.

Sometimes I work very
hard to prove that I
am free

but I am not free

and I know it.

Sometimes I think I am free and I want others to stop using controllers.

Then I discover that I am trying to become a controller myself.

As I learn to live without controllers, I feel less of a need to control others.

There are times when
someone near me isn't
using controllers.

This makes it harder for me to use my controllers and I am frightened

so I try to create controllers

for the other person.

After collecting controllers
for a long time, I have more
controllers than I can ever
use

None of my controllers
will really be responsible
for my behavior.

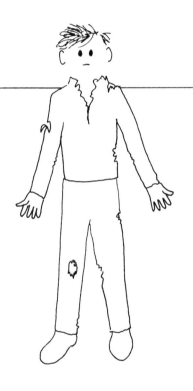

I alone am responsible
for my behavior.

There is no one to take the responsibility for my behavior.

There never really was.

The more I take the
responsibility for my own
behavior,

the more I want
the responsibility and the
less I use the controllers.

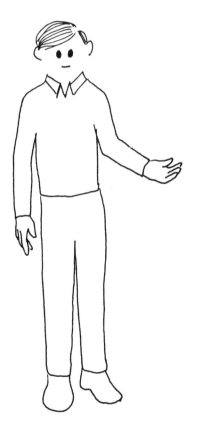

Sometimes I am free.

My being responsible
may make another person
feel uncertain

so the other person tries

to create controllers for me.

It doesn't work because I am
the only person who can
ever create controllers for
me.

The more I live

without controllers

the more I grow to

understand that

I am free

only when

I am responsible.

THE FACSADE
A VIEW OF OUR BEHAVIOR

BY
JIM
COLE

Other Books
by
Jim Cole

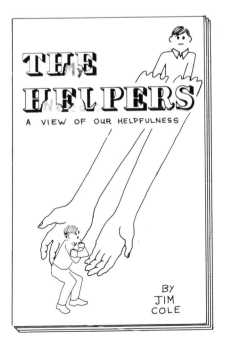

THE HELPERS
A VIEW OF OUR HELPFULNESS

BY
JIM
COLE